**Biff, Chip & Kipper**

# Stories and Activities

Series created by
**Roderick Hunt & Alex Brychta**

Activities written by
**Isabel Thomas**

OXFORD
UNIVERSITY PRESS

# Tips for reading

Sharing stories is one of the best ways to help children learn to read. The two *Biff, Chip and Kipper* stories featured in this book are a springboard to fun activities that will help your child to practise sounds, letters and early reading skills at home.

## Making learning fun

Both stories have familiar characters and settings to build your child's vocabulary and knowledge about the world. The themed activities provide opportunities to talk about the stories and will help your child to develop important skills for reading and writing.

You'll also find ideas for games and activities to continue the fun after you've finished each section.

The best way to encourage your child is to offer lots of praise. When they complete the book, help them to find the matching reward sticker. Then, when they get to the end of the book, they can complete the 'well done' certificate on page 32.

Children learn best when they are having fun. Find a time to read with your child when they are not too tired or distracted. At **Read with Oxford Stage 2** children should be able to concentrate on activities for about 10 minutes.

## Enjoying the activities

Each time you return to the book, share the story again before you start the activities. Children enjoy re-reading stories and this gentle reminder helps to build their confidence and will make the activities fun and easier to complete.

## Before reading

Read the title of the story together and look at the pictures. Ask your child what they think the story is about.

Before you read the stories, show your child these letter patterns. Say the sounds they make.

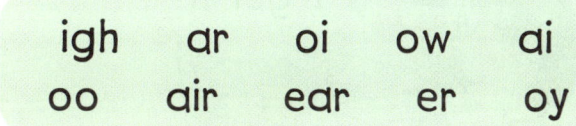

| igh | ar | oi | ow | ai |
| oo | air | ear | er | oy |

You can listen to the letter sounds at **oxfordowl.co.uk**

Practise blending the sounds to make these words. Say the sounds in each word, then blend the sounds together to make the word (e.g. *Ch-ip, Chip*).

### Story 1
zip   Chip   duck   shop
coins   wow   boy

### Story 2
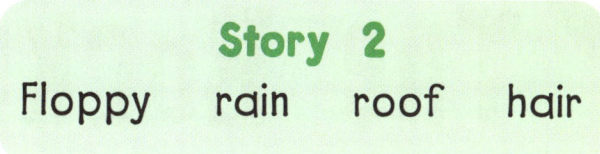

Floppy   rain   roof   hair

## Tricky words

'Tricky words', or 'common exception words', are words which do not follow the phonics rules that your child will be learning in school. Your child may need help with these tricky words. Say them together before you start reading.

### Story 1
was   put   by   the
I'll   said

### Story 2
my   so   no   go   to

When you come across these words in the stories, remind your child they are tricky words that they need to recognise. Encourage your child to have a go at saying them out loud. Say the word for them if they struggle.

## 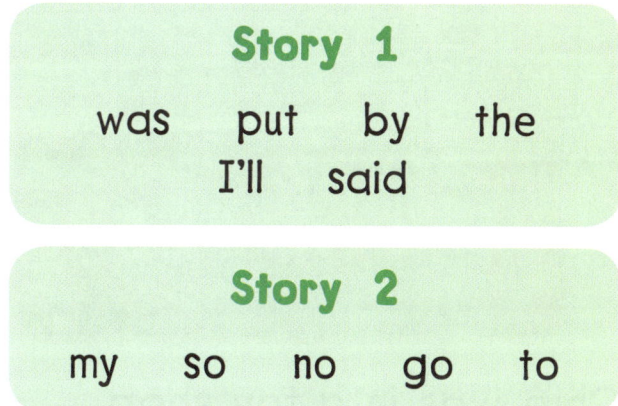 Oxford Owl

The Oxford Owl website is packed full of resources to help support your child's learning at home. Visit **oxfordowl.co.uk** to find more activities, free eBooks, information on the **Read with Oxford Stages** and other practical advice to help your child progress with reading.

Enjoy the stories!

# The Backpack

Written by **Roderick Hunt**
Illustrated by **Alex Brychta**

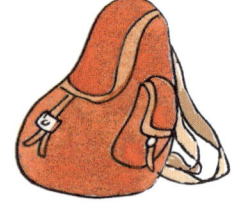

Chip was in a toy shop.

He put his backpack by the ducks.

A boy put his backpack by the ducks.

"Look at this rocket," said Chip.

**5**

In the zip pocket.

"My coins are in my backpack," he said.

**6**

Mum got a backpack.

**7**

But it was not Chip's backpack.

**8**

Pick it up, Nick.

The boy had Chip's backpack.

Chip had the boy's backpack.

Chip was upset.

"Let's get them back," said Mum.

Mum and Chip ran ...

... to this shop ...
... to that shop.

**14**

The boy got on a bus.

**15**

"Stop that bus," said Mum.

**16**

The bus did stop.

**17**

Chip got his backpack back.

Find four mice hidden in the pictures.

# New letter Sounds

What did Chip say when he saw all the toys? Do you like visiting toy shops?

**1** **Say** the letter sounds. **Name** the pictures.
**Join** each picture to the right sound.

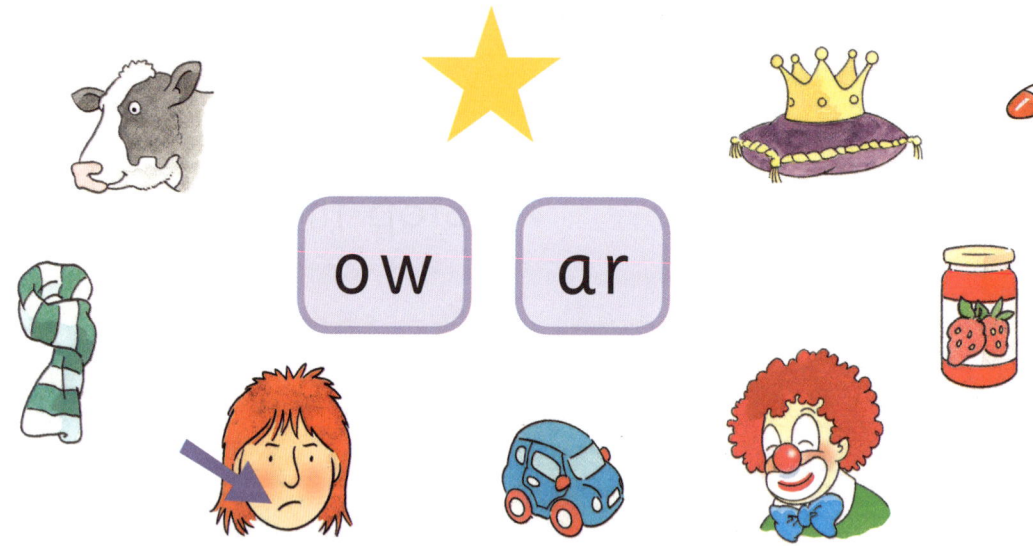

o w    a r

**2** What is each character saying?
**Join** the pictures to the right speech bubbles.

Wow!    Ow!    Pow!

**3** Some toys make noises. **Say** the sounds.
**Choose** a toy sticker to put next to each bubble.

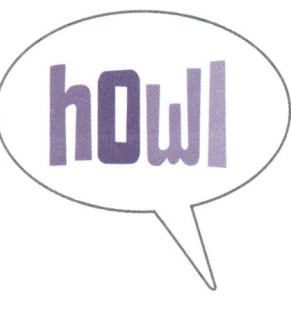

**Try this!**

Teach your child the phrase *How now brown cow*? Can you and your child make up any more phrases using words that rhyme?

# Alternative letter sounds

Where did Chip put his backpack while he looked at the toys? Was it safe?

## 1 Say the sounds. Trace and write the letters.

c c ___  k k ___  ck ck ___

## 2 Choose a letter sound to complete each word.

c  k  ck

 __ ing

so ___

 __ lock

po ___ et

 __ ap

chi ___ en

**3** **Use** the stickers. **Put** each toy next to its label.

| duck | truck | rocket |

**4** Both of these letter patterns make the same sound. **Say** the sound. **Trace** and write the letters.

oi o̤i̤ _____     oy o̤y̤ _____

**5** **Draw** a line to join each toy to the right coins.

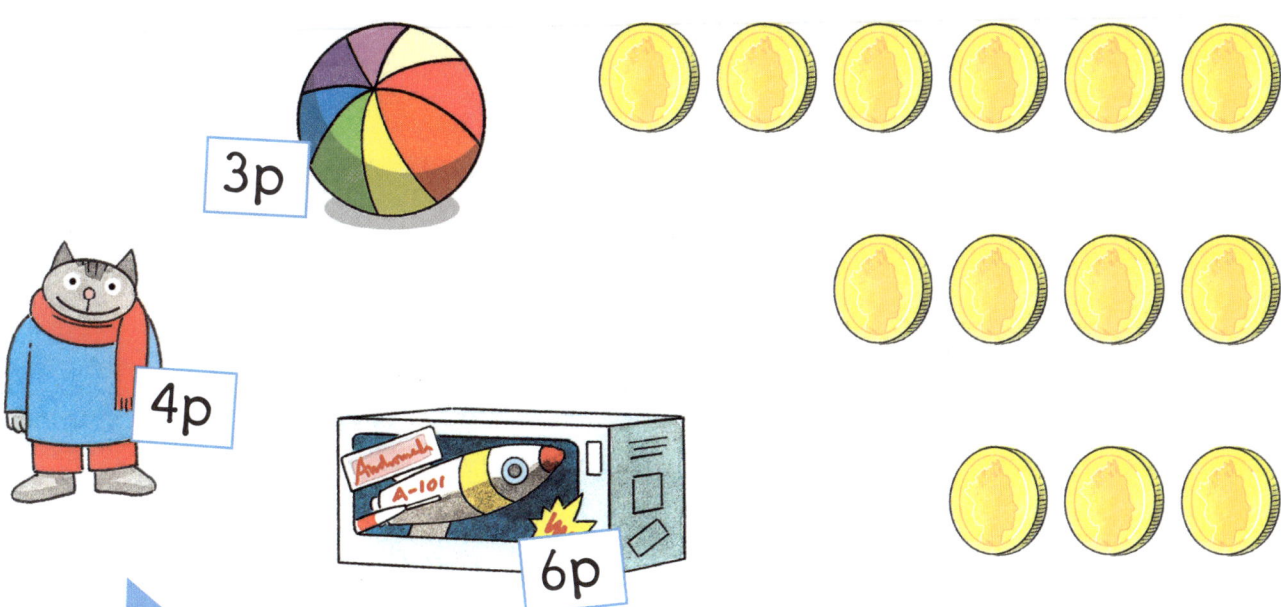

3p

4p

6p

**Try this!**

When your child is learning a new letter sound, ask them to make a 3D version out of play dough or building blocks. They can trace the shape with their finger while saying the sound.

# Blending sounds

Where were Chip's coins?
Why was Chip worried?
Why did Nick pick up
Chip's backpack?

**1** **Underline** the letters in each word that make the sound /**oi**/. **Blend** the sounds together to say the words.

boil       oil      boy      toy

**2** Chip and Nick made a list of the things in their backpacks. **Add** the right stickers to each backpack.

coins

jar

party hat

toy owl

cap

book

art set

toy car

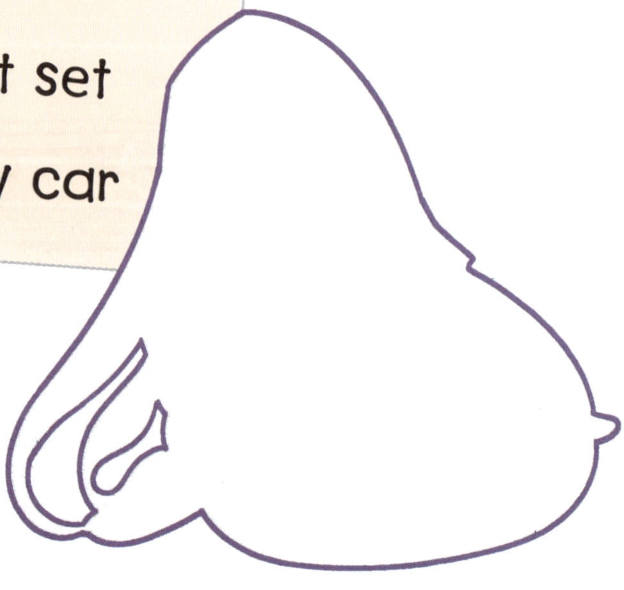

**3** **Join** each person to the shop they need.

I need garlic.

cook shop

I need party hats.

barber

I need a garden fork.

market

I need a haircut.

party shop

I need a pan.

garden shop

Try this!

Ask your child to design a toy alien. They could draw it, or make it out of play dough or building blocks. Ask them to make up an alien name, and try to write it down.

# Spelling words

Draw your favourite toy and write its name.

**1** **Write** the missing letter patterns on Mum's shopping list. **Add** the stickers to the shopping basket.

ow    ar    or

j__ of sweets

f__my__d

cl__n

t__ch

**2** **Complete** each word with **oi** or **oy**.

dig the s__l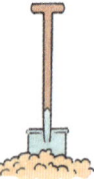

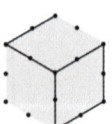 j__n the dots

look at the cowb__

enj__ the party

14

**3** **Choose** one letter pattern from each basket to help you write a label for each toy.

Basket 1: sh, c, ch

Basket 2: i, ee, ar, e

Basket 3: p, d, ss

| sh | i | p |
| --- | --- | --- |

| | | |
| --- | --- | --- |

| | | |
| --- | --- | --- |

| | | |
| --- | --- | --- |

**Try this!**

When you are writing a shopping list, pause from time to time and ask your child to help you spell a word by telling you which letters to write. Ask them to write their own shopping lists, too.

# Reading captions

How did Chip get his backpack back? Have you ever lost something precious? Where did you find it?

**1** **Circle** the right word to finish each caption.

Mum and Chip ran down the town / street.

Chip got his backpack / rocket back.

**2** The toy shop is a mess! **Read** the captions. **Add** the stickers in the right place.

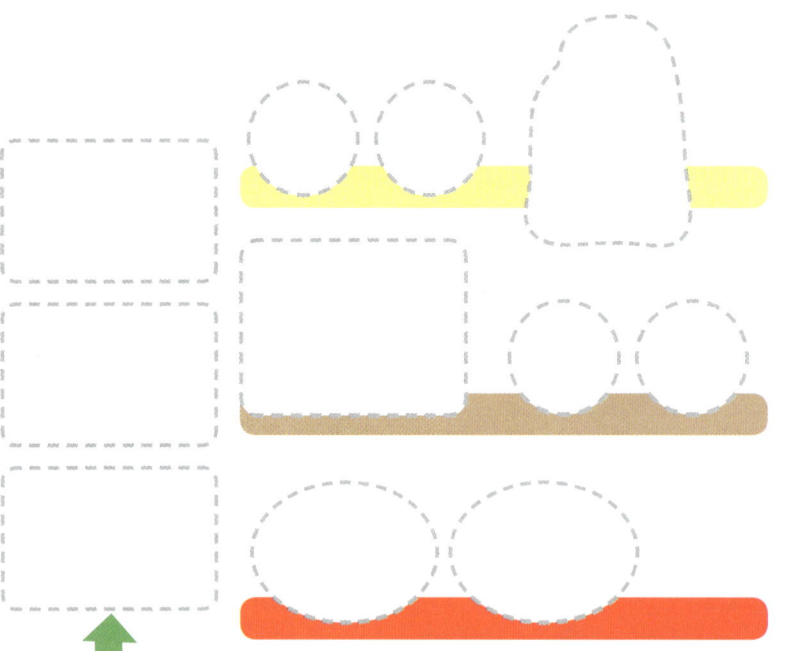

Put the cat on the top shelf.

Put the truck on the brown shelf.

Put two balls on the brown shelf.

Stack the ducks up.

Park the cars on the red shelf.

Put two balls on the top shelf.

# Page 9

# Page 11

# Page 12

# Page 16

# Page 14

Page 17

Page 22

Page 23

Page 26

Page 29

Page 31

Page 32

**3** Take it in turns with a partner to **roll** a dice and **read** a word. Each time you read a word, **cover** it up with a counter. The first person to make a row of three counters (across or down) wins the game!

You need:
- a dice
- 24 small counters or squares of paper, in two colours.

| coil | port | boy | market | town | sharp |
|---|---|---|---|---|---|
| oil | orbit | joy | dark | howl | torch |
| poison | for | annoy | charm | cow | harsh |
| tinfoil | cornet | enjoy | hard | towel | short |

Each time you complete the game, have a reward sticker!

**Try this!** Write simple clues to create a treasure hunt for your child, e.g. *go to the shed, look on the shelf, lift up the rug.*

17

# Rain Again

Written by **Roderick Hunt**
Illustrated by **Nick Schon**

Rain again, rain again.

Get in my den.

Rain on the roof.

Rain in my den.

**5**

Get a pail.

**6**

Rain again, rain again.

**7**

Rain in my shed.

**8**

Fix the roof.

So much rain.

Rain again, rain again.

So much rain.

Rain in my boots.

I am wet, wet, wet.

**14**

Rain in my hair.

**15**

But I am not wet.

**17**

No, Floppy!

**16**

Floppy is wet.

**18**

Find five brown birds in the pictures.

# New letter sounds

Talk about the story. Why does Chip ask Kipper to get a pail?

**1** **Say** the sounds. **Trace** and **write** the letters.

ai ai _____     oa oa _____

**2** **Use** the stickers. **Put** the objects in the right buckets.

/oa/     /ai/     other

**3** **Say** the sounds. **Trace** and **write** the letters.

oo oo _____     er er _____

**4** **Read** the labels. **Add** the stickers.

| ladder | hammer |

| nails | boots | broom |

**5** **Draw** lines to match the labels to the pictures.

| wet | wetter | wettest |

Turn tidying up into a blending game. Sound-talk the name of an object that needs tidying up, e.g. *f-oo-t-b-all b-oo-t-s*. Ask your child to blend the sounds and then tidy up that object. Give a reward sticker each time you play.

*Try this!*

# Three letters, one sound

What are the different ways that the characters try to keep dry? Does the umbrella keep Kipper dry?

**1** Sometimes three letters make one sound.
**Say** the sounds. **Write** the letter patterns, e.g. **igh**.

**igh** as in high _____

**air** as in hair _____

**ear** as in hear _____

**2** **Name** the objects. **Join** each picture to the right sound.

/**igh**/    /**air**/    /**ear**/

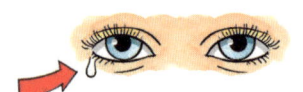

  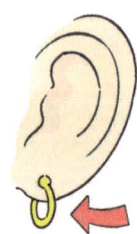    

**3** **Read** the rhyme in Chip's book. **Draw** a line underneath three letters that make one sound.

One dark night, I hear a growl.

What a fright! Don't look now.

Small ears, brown hair ...

Oh dear! It's a ...

**4** Is it right? **Read** the questions. **Circle** *yes* or *no*.

Are three things a pair? yes / no

Is it light at night? yes / no

Do dogs sleep at night? yes / no

Is a day longer than a year? yes / no

Can you hear a car right now? yes / no

Encourage your child to read signs in shops, on buses and trains, and in waiting rooms. It's a good way to introduce them to a wide range of new words.

Try this!

# Reading words and Captions

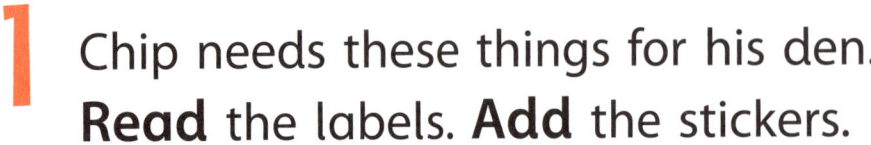

Have you ever built a den? Where did you build it? What did you use?

**1** Chip needs these things for his den.
**Read** the labels. **Add** the stickers.

sticks

wood

ladder

nails

paint

hammer

**2** Help Kipper get dressed to play in the rain.
**Tick** each thing when you have coloured it in.

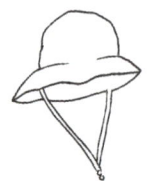

rain hat ☐

umbrella ☐

boots ☐

raincoat ☐

**3** **Read** the instructions. **Draw** a den.
**Write** your name on the banner.

How to put up a reading den

1. Get two chairs.

2. Put them far apart.

3. Add a sheet for a roof.

4. Then, add some books.

_____

**4** **Join** each caption to the right picture.

Then I fill my
den with books.

I will need a
torch to read.

This den will
need a roof.

Help your child to build a reading den in the house or garden. You could drape a sheet over a table or washing line, or use an old cardboard box. Add some cushions and snuggle up to read a book!

# Writing words

Why are Kipper and his family laughing at the end?

**1** Floppy has splashed some of the words.
**Choose** the letter patterns to finish each caption.

air   ear   igh   oo

- Mum has f____h____.

- Oh d____! There is

  rain in my h____.

- A frog z____ms out

  of Dad's b____t

- Hold t____t or you

  m____t get wet!

28

## 2 **Say** the words. **Write** each letter in the right box.

Across

1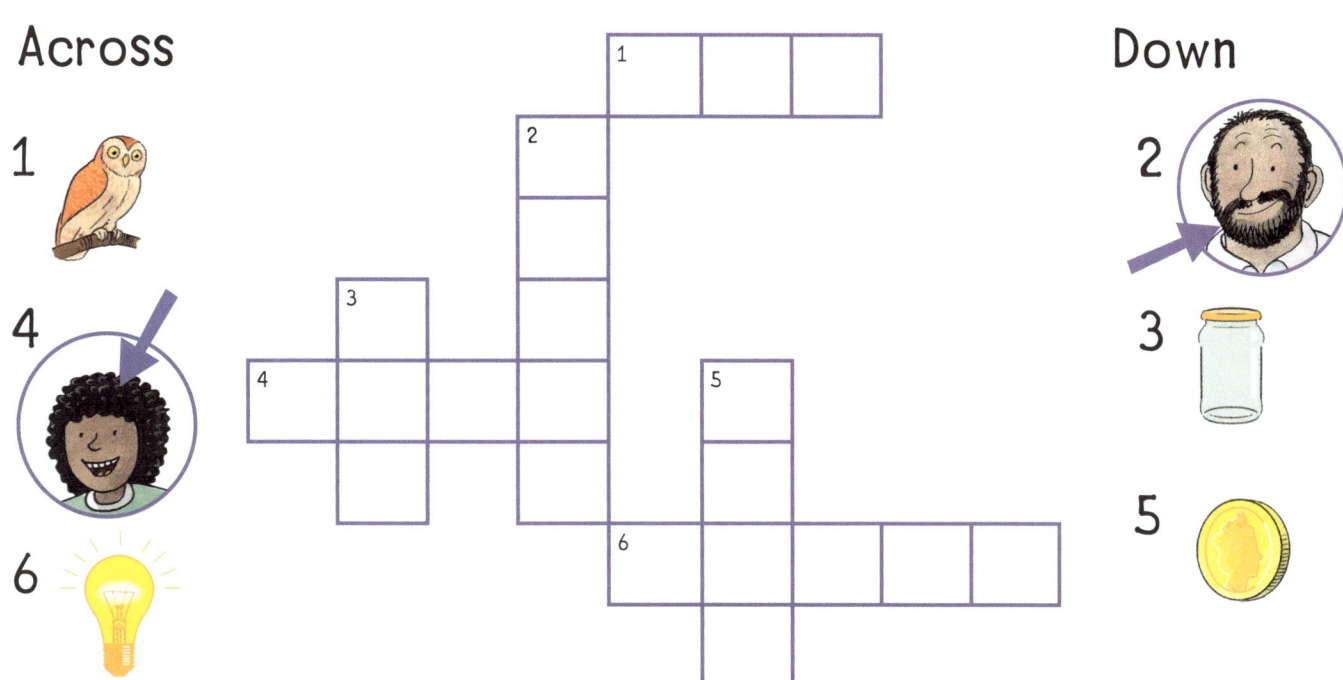

4

6

Down

2

3

5

## 3 **Use** the stickers to finish the picture. **Add** the missing letters to each label.

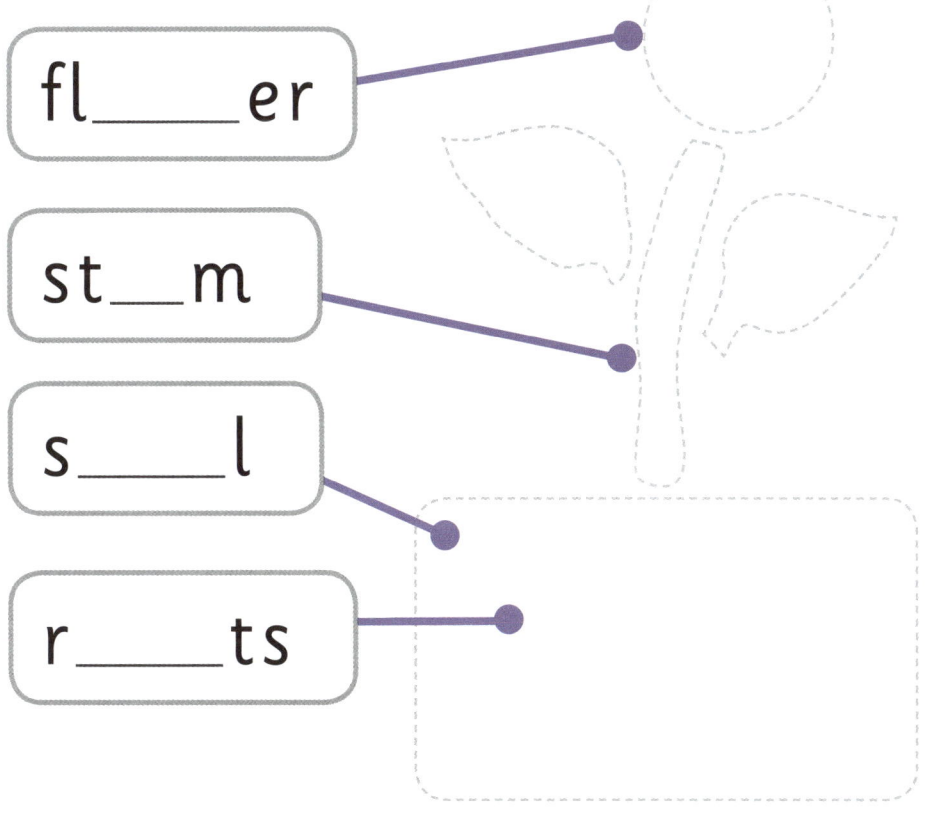

fl___er

st__m

s___l

r___ts

**Try this!**

As your child learns more letter patterns, encourage them to add simple labels to pictures that they draw.

# Tricky words

What do you like to do when it's raining?

## 1 Join each caption to the right picture.

He has a hammer and a nail.

She will need a towel.

Mum will brush her hair.

Floppy wags his tail.

## 2 Write a caption for this picture.

**3** With a partner, **play** bingo with tricky words.
**Write** the 12 words in the grid on scraps of paper.
**Choose** a grid. **Take turns** to pull a word out of
a hat. If you can find the word on your grid, **cover**
it with a counter or a small toy. When they are all
covered, call 'bingo'!

| | |
|---|---|
| he | be |
| you | all |
| they | was |

| | |
|---|---|
| she | me |
| we | are |
| her | my |

Each time you complete
the game, have a
reward sticker!

_____

has completed the

# Stories and Activities

Date _____ , 20_____

## OXFORD
### UNIVERSITY PRESS

Great Clarendon Street, Oxford, OX2 6DP, United Kingdom

Oxford University Press is a department of the University of Oxford. It furthers the University's objective of excellence in research, scholarship, and education by publishing worldwide. Oxford is a registered trade mark of Oxford University Press in the UK and in certain other countries

Activity pages text © Oxford University Press 2018

The Backpack, Rain Again text © Roderick Hunt 2007

The Backpack illustrations © Alex Brychta 2007

Rain Again illustrations © Nick Schon 2007

The Backpack, Rain Again first published in 2007

The characters in this work are the original creation of Roderick Hunt and Alex Brychta who retain copyright in the characters.

Activities written by Isabel Thomas

The moral rights of the author have been asserted

First published in 2018

British Library Cataloguing in Publication Data
Data available

ISBN: 978-0-19-276467-6

10 9 8 7 6 5 4 3 2 1

Paper used in the production of this book is a natural, recyclable product made from wood grown in sustainable forests. The manufacturing process conforms to the environmental regulations of the country of origin.

Printed in China

### Acknowledgements

Series Editor: Annemarie Young

Activity pages additional artwork by Stuart Trotter